This Handsome Man Belongs To

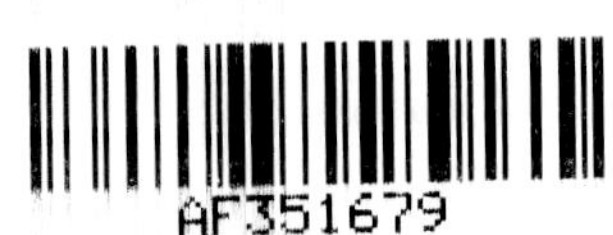

____

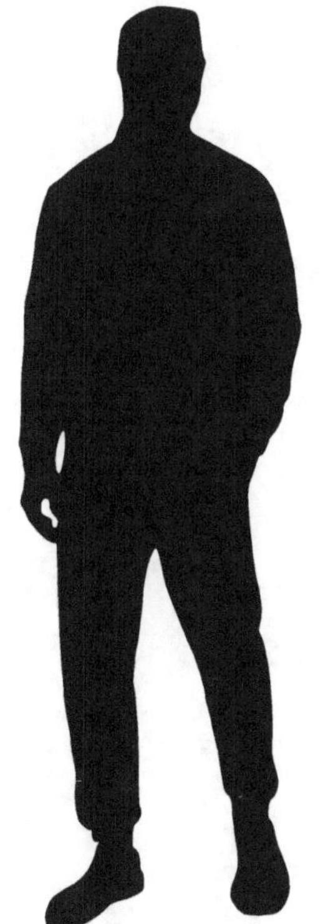

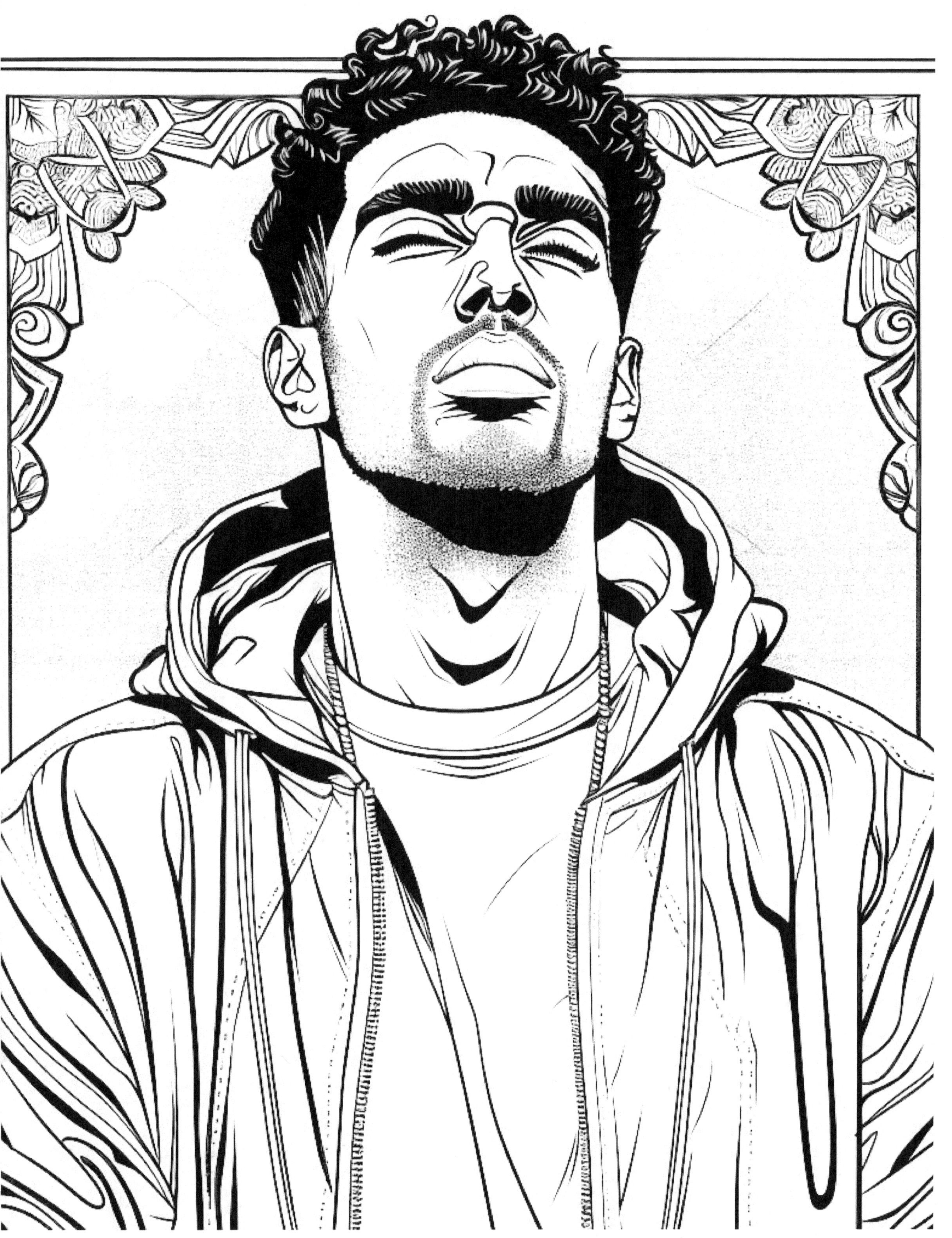

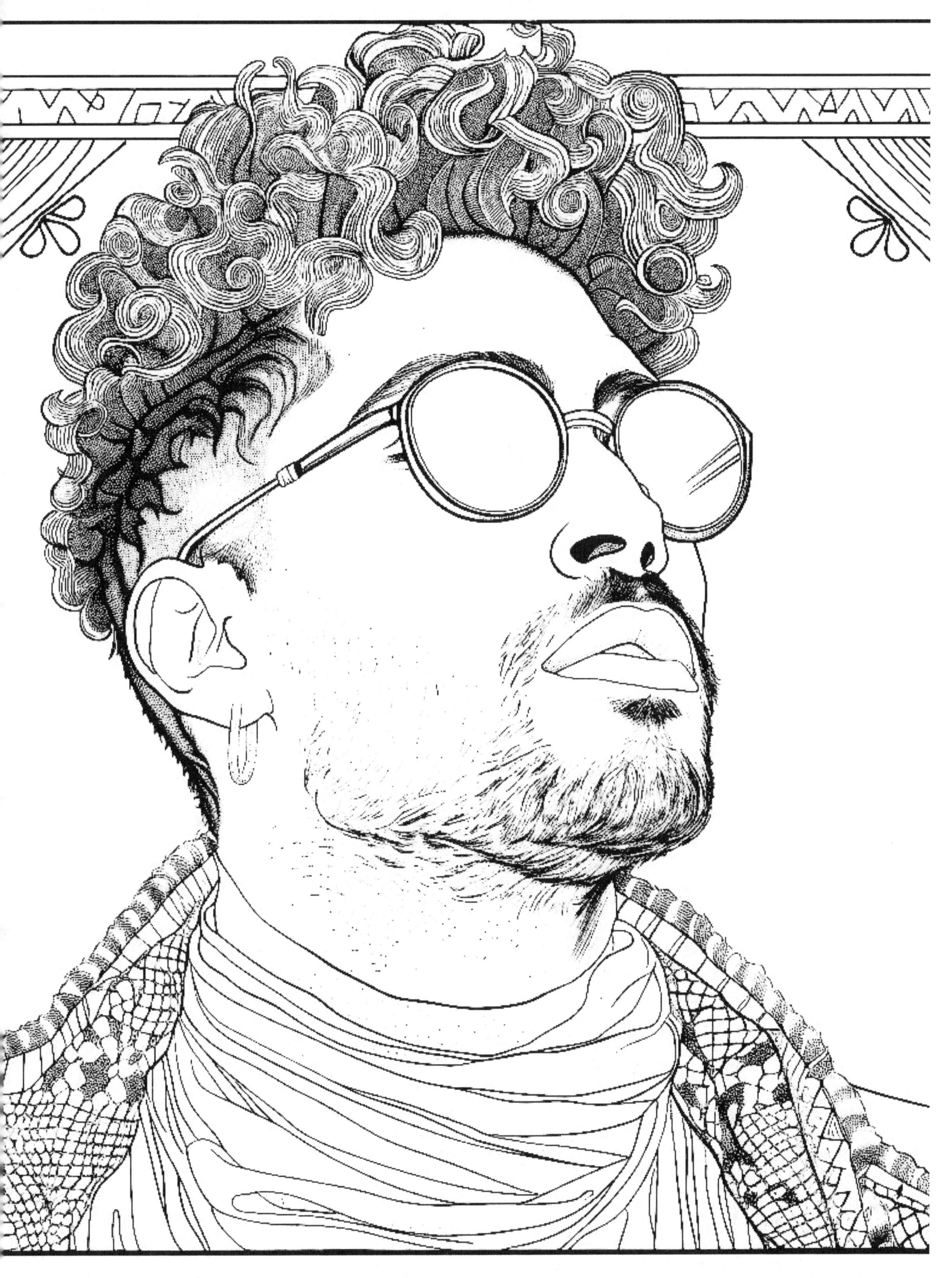

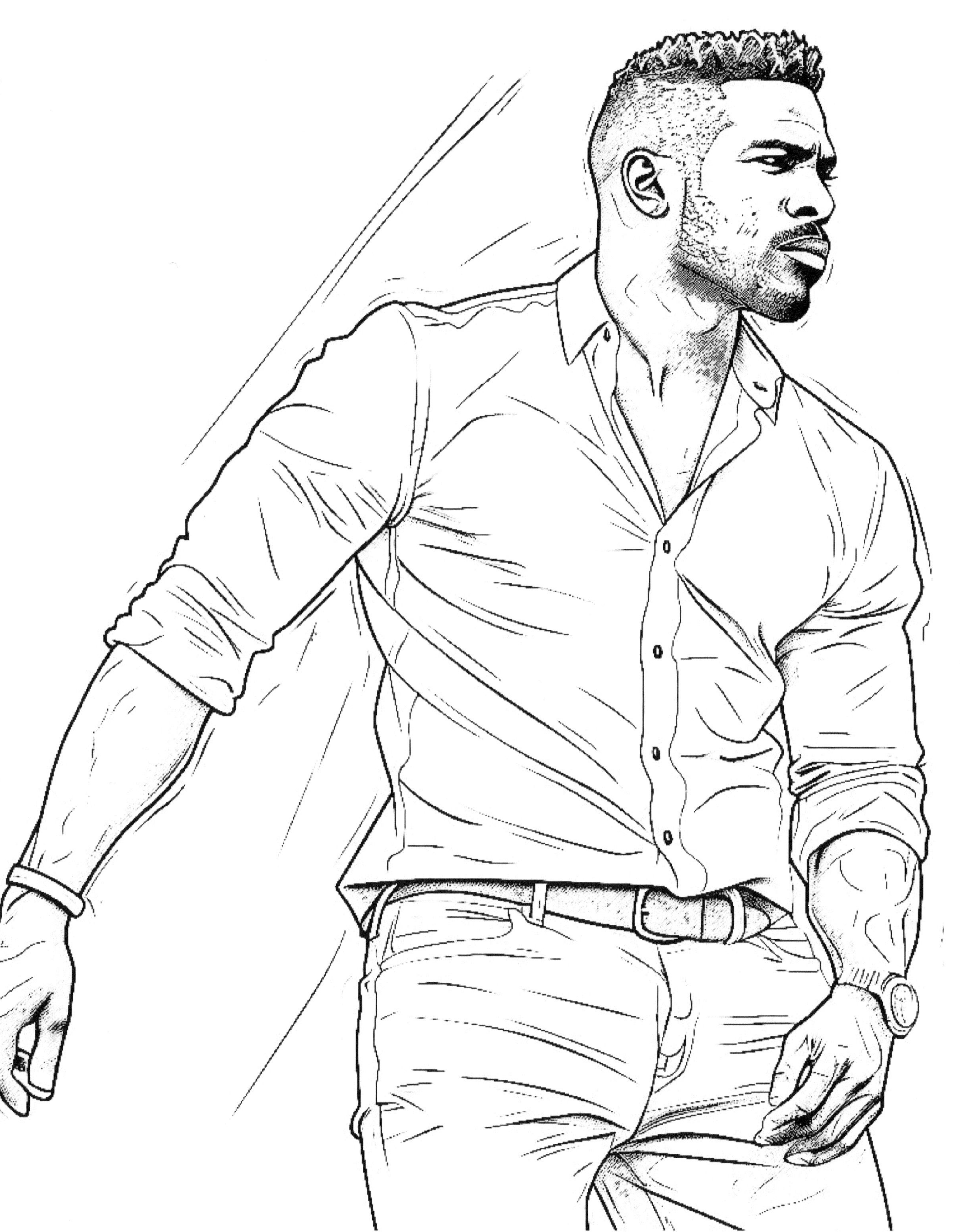

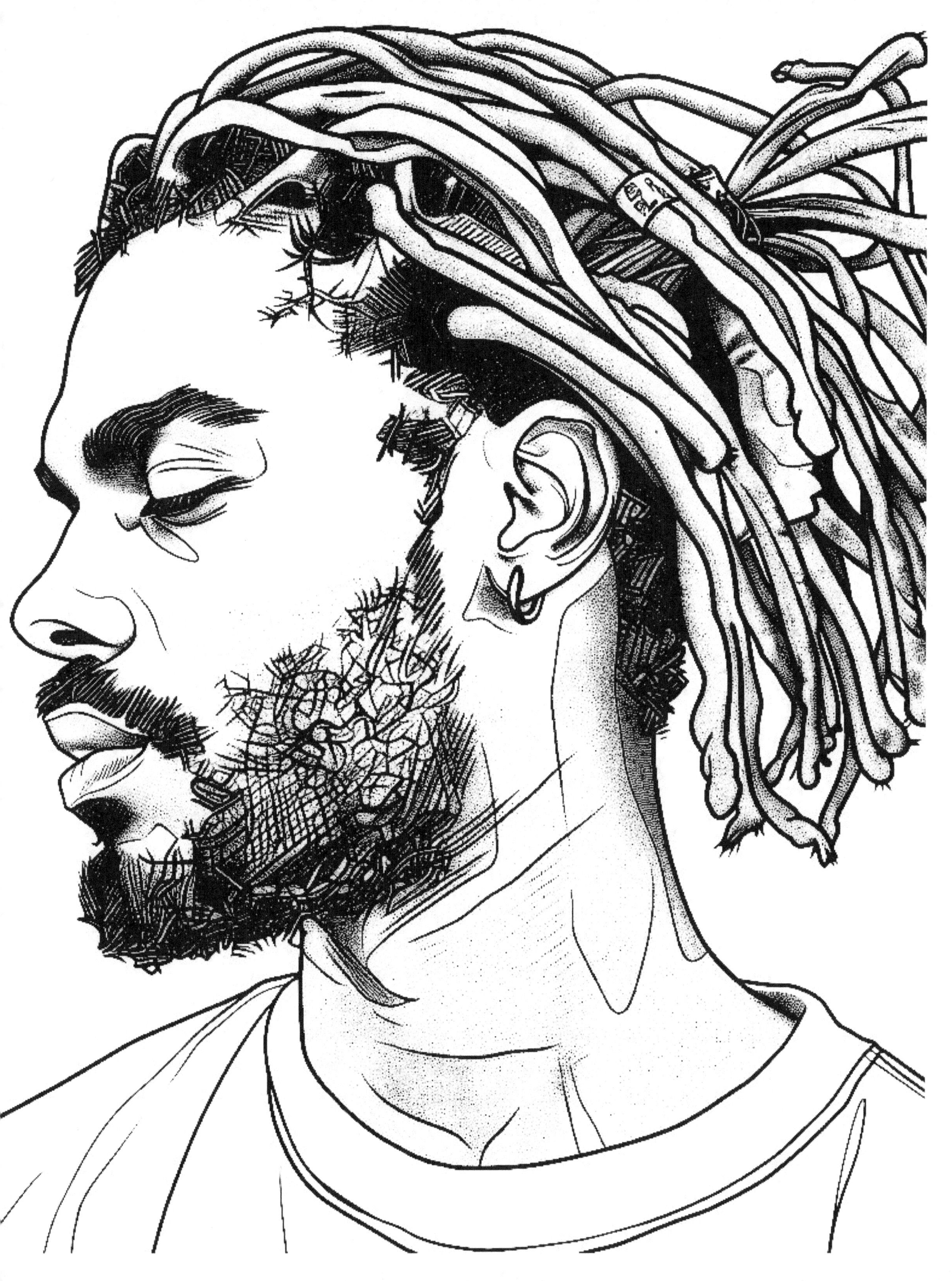

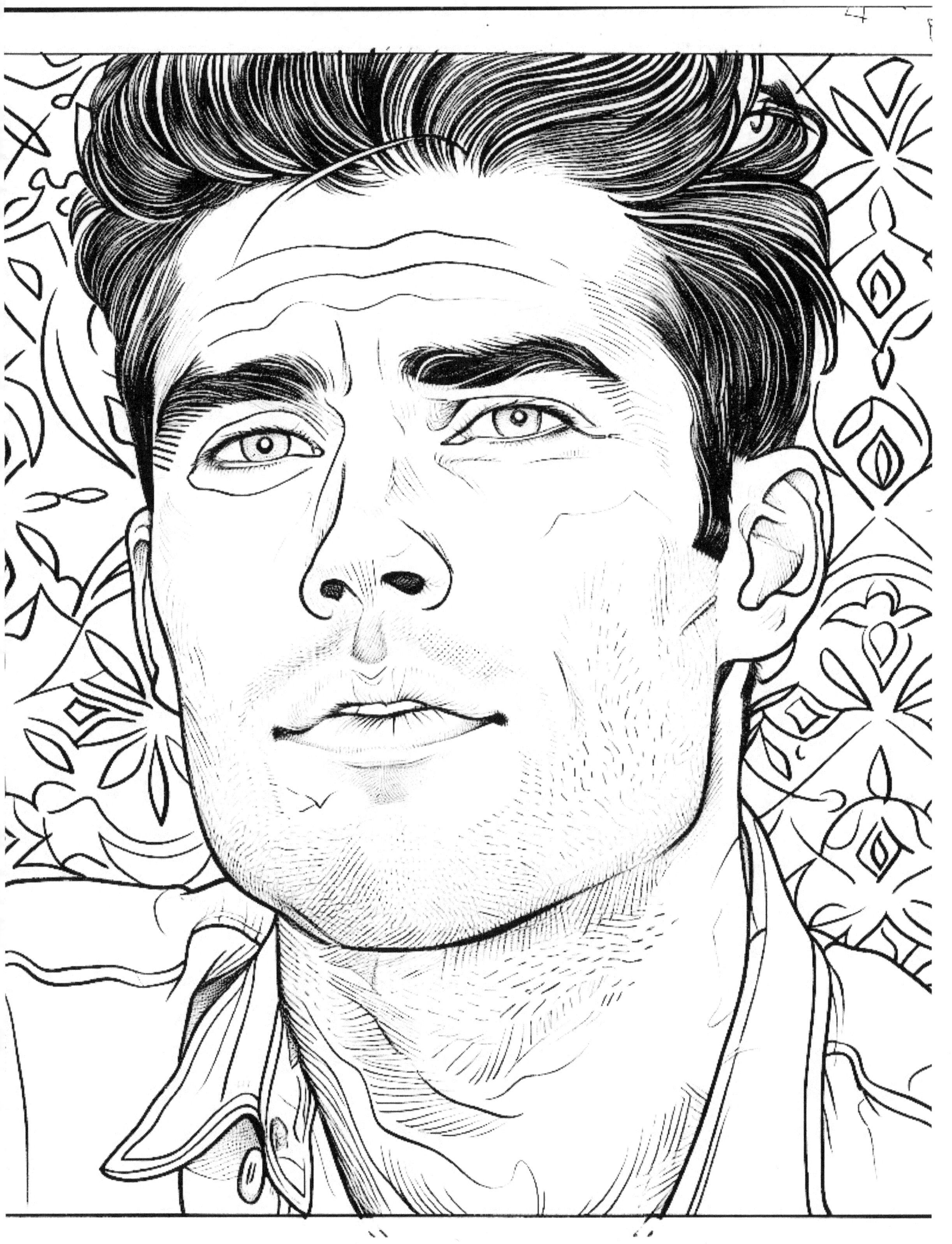

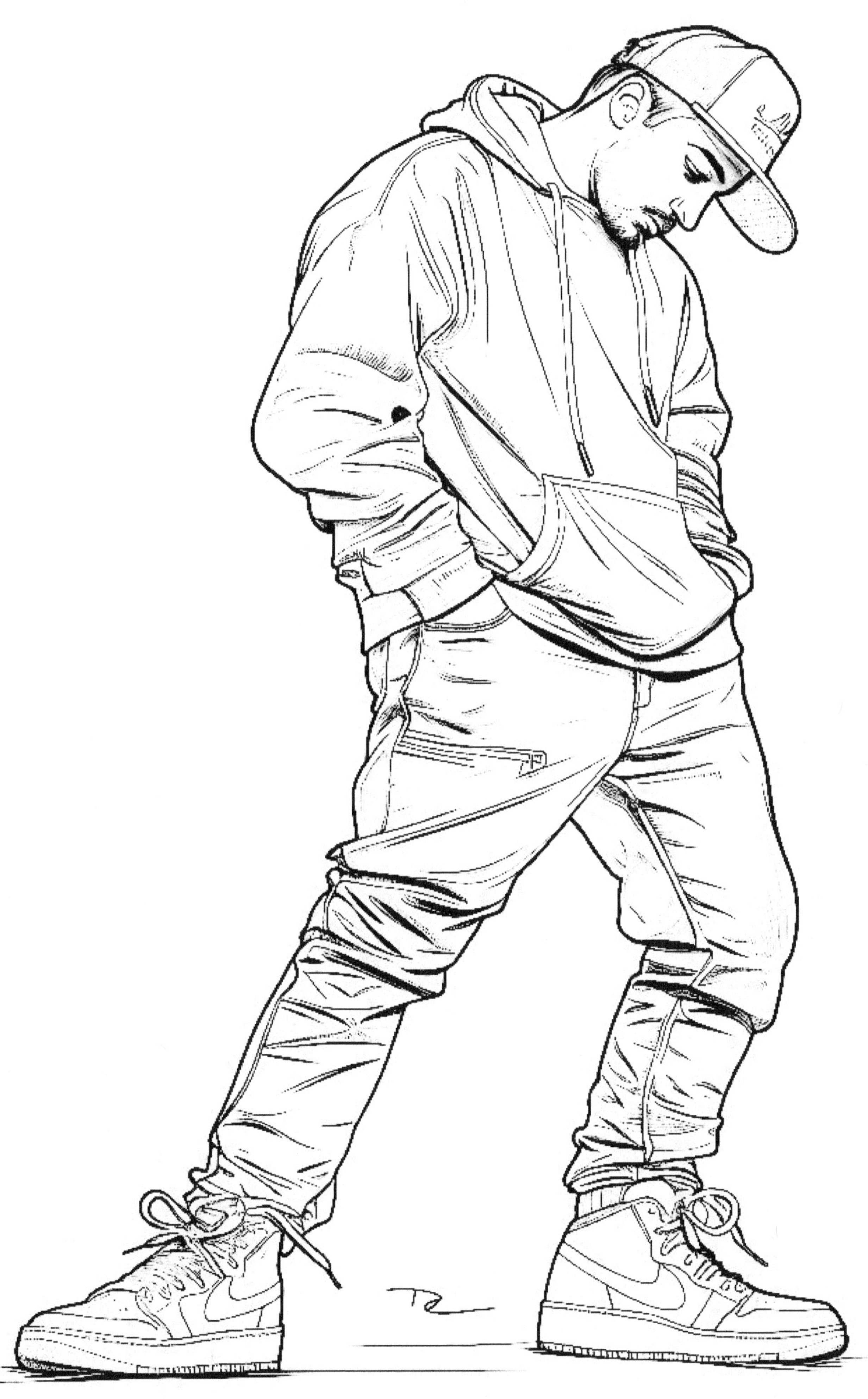

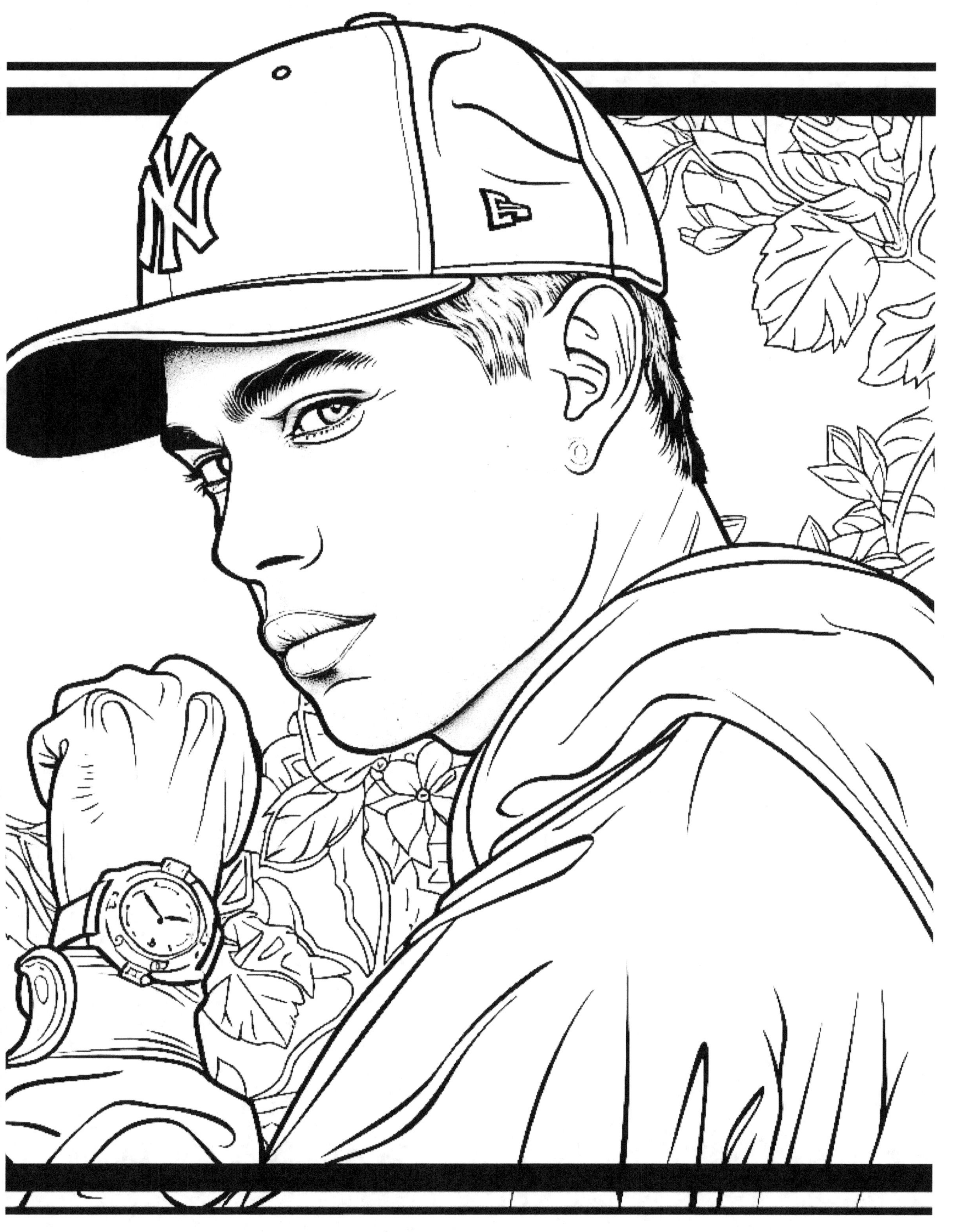

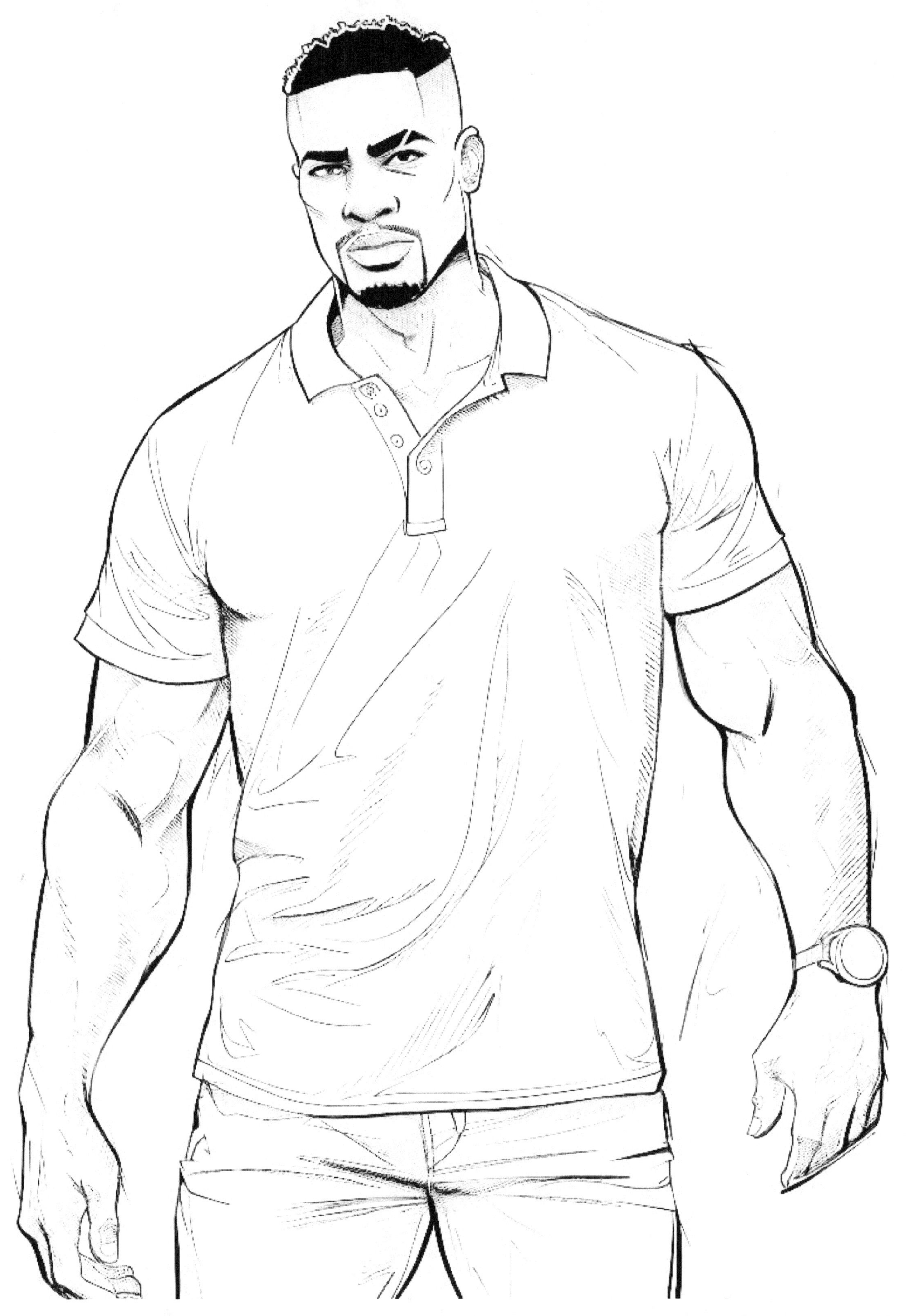

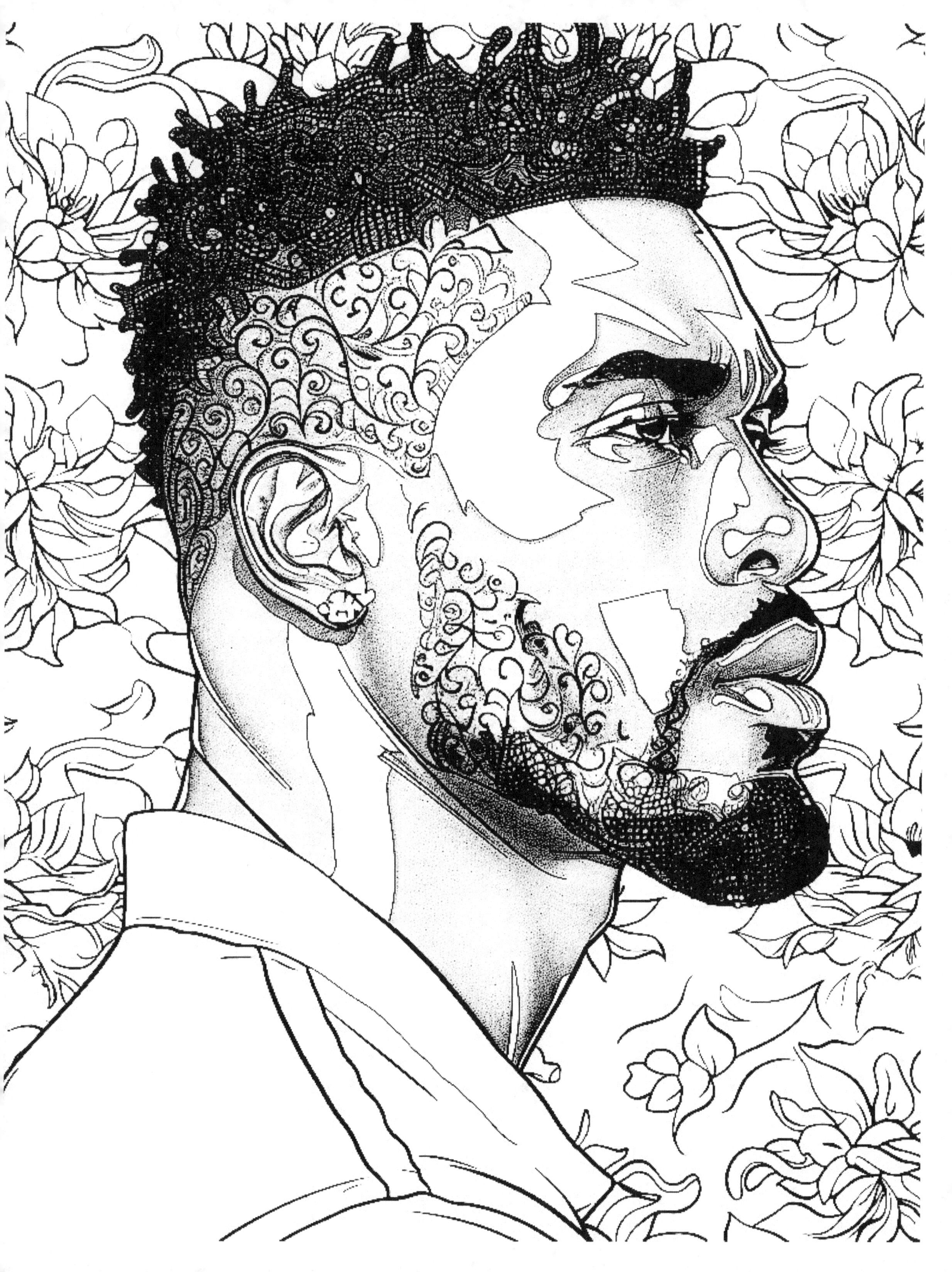

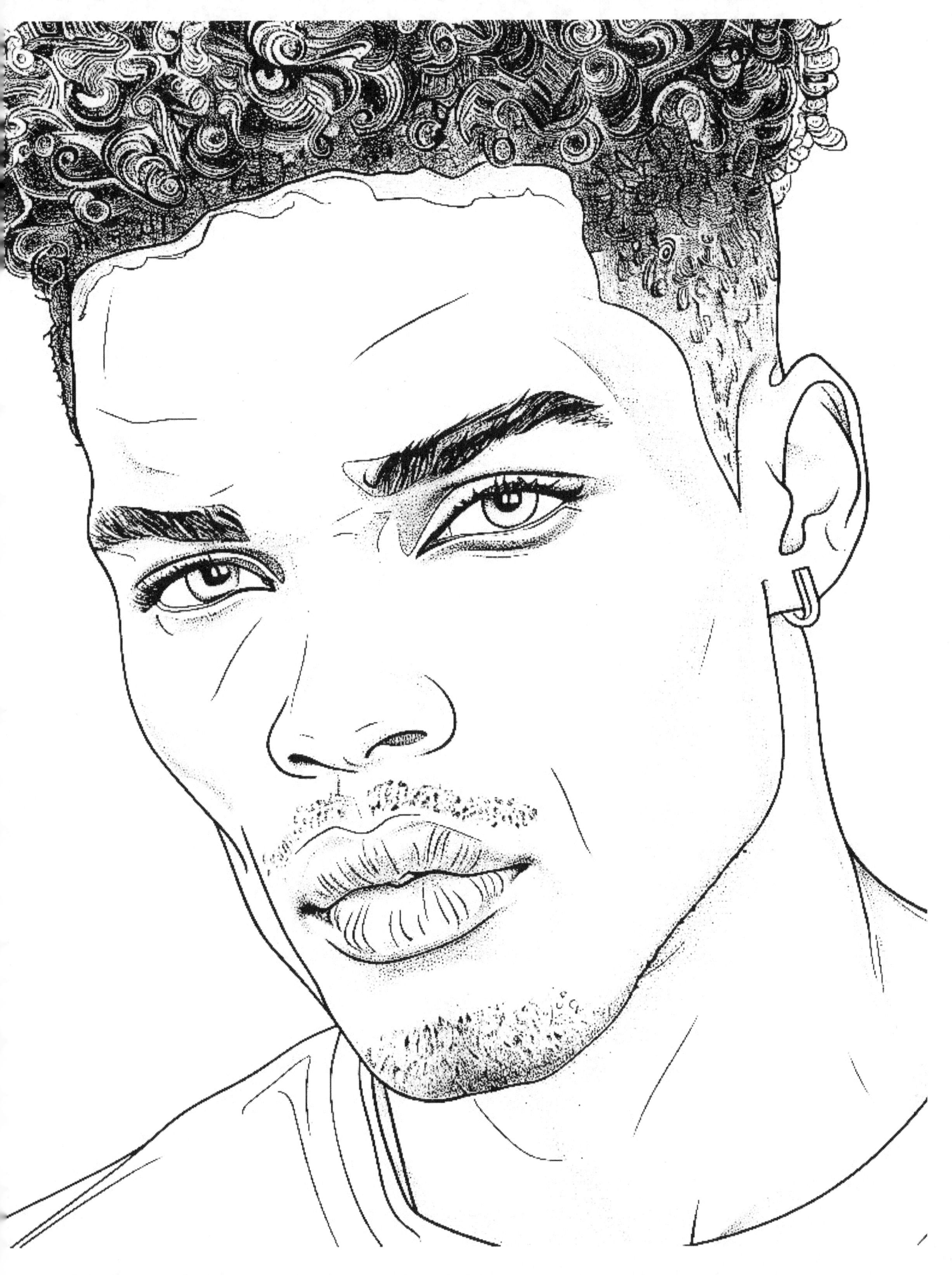

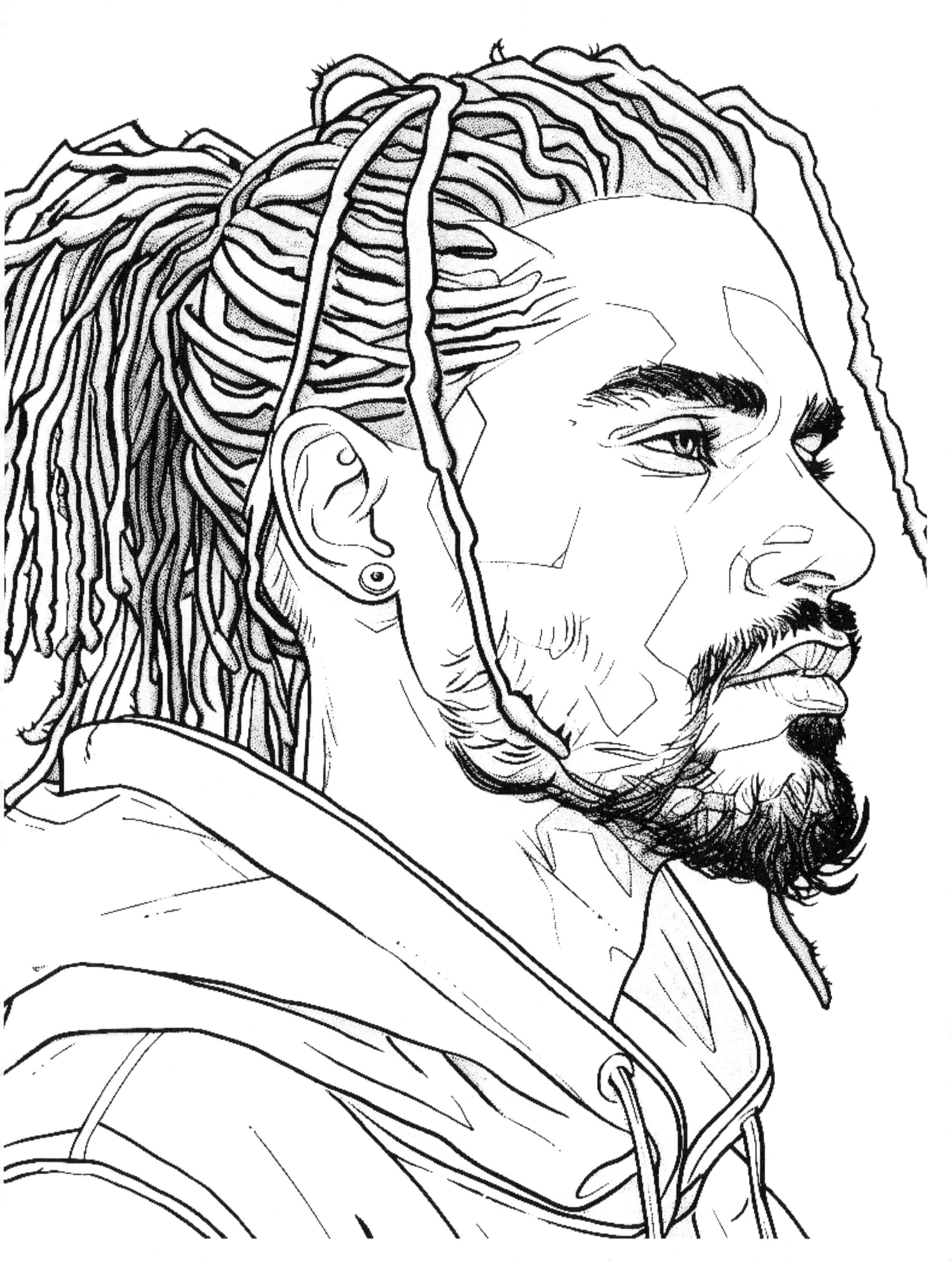

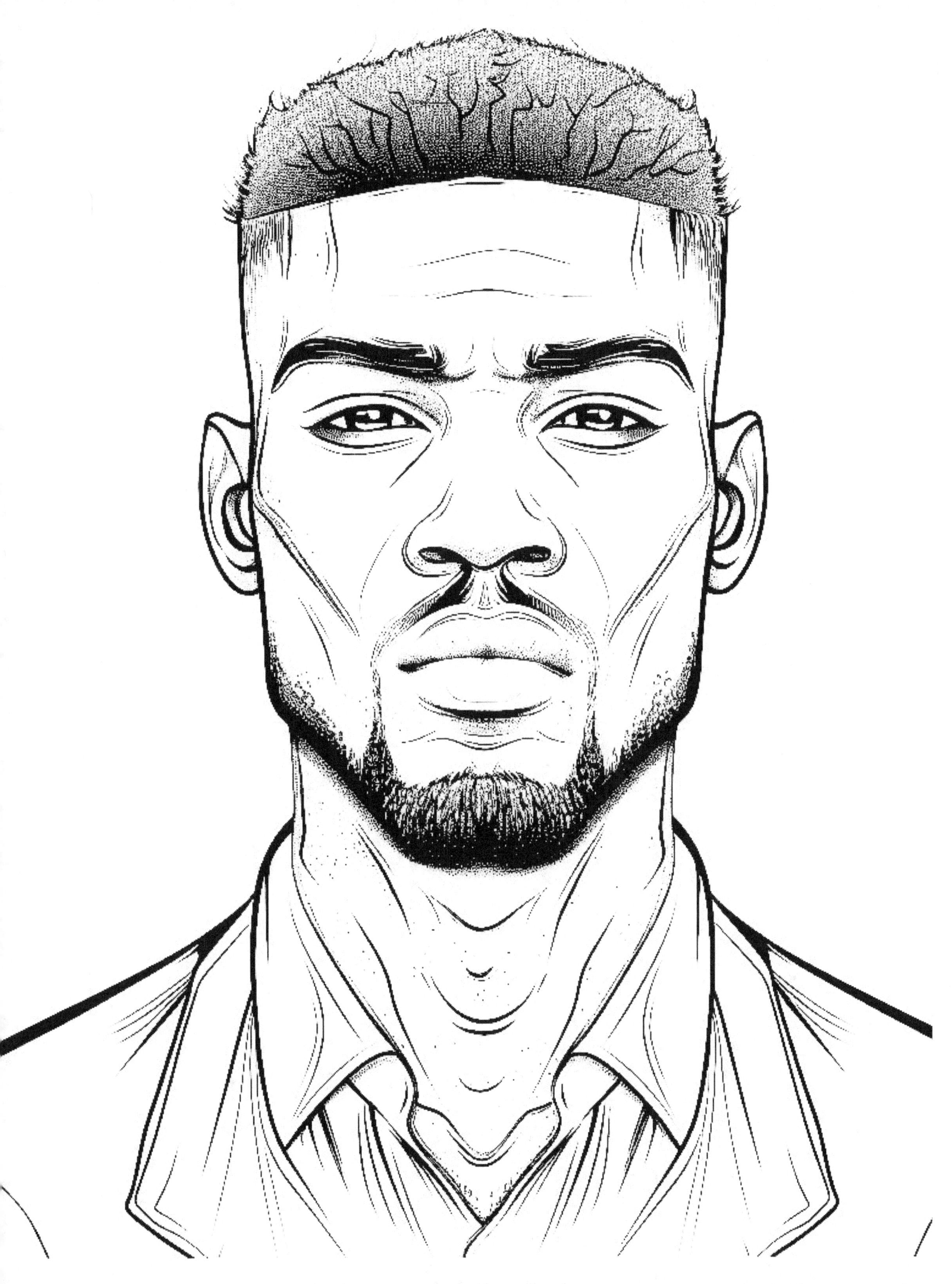

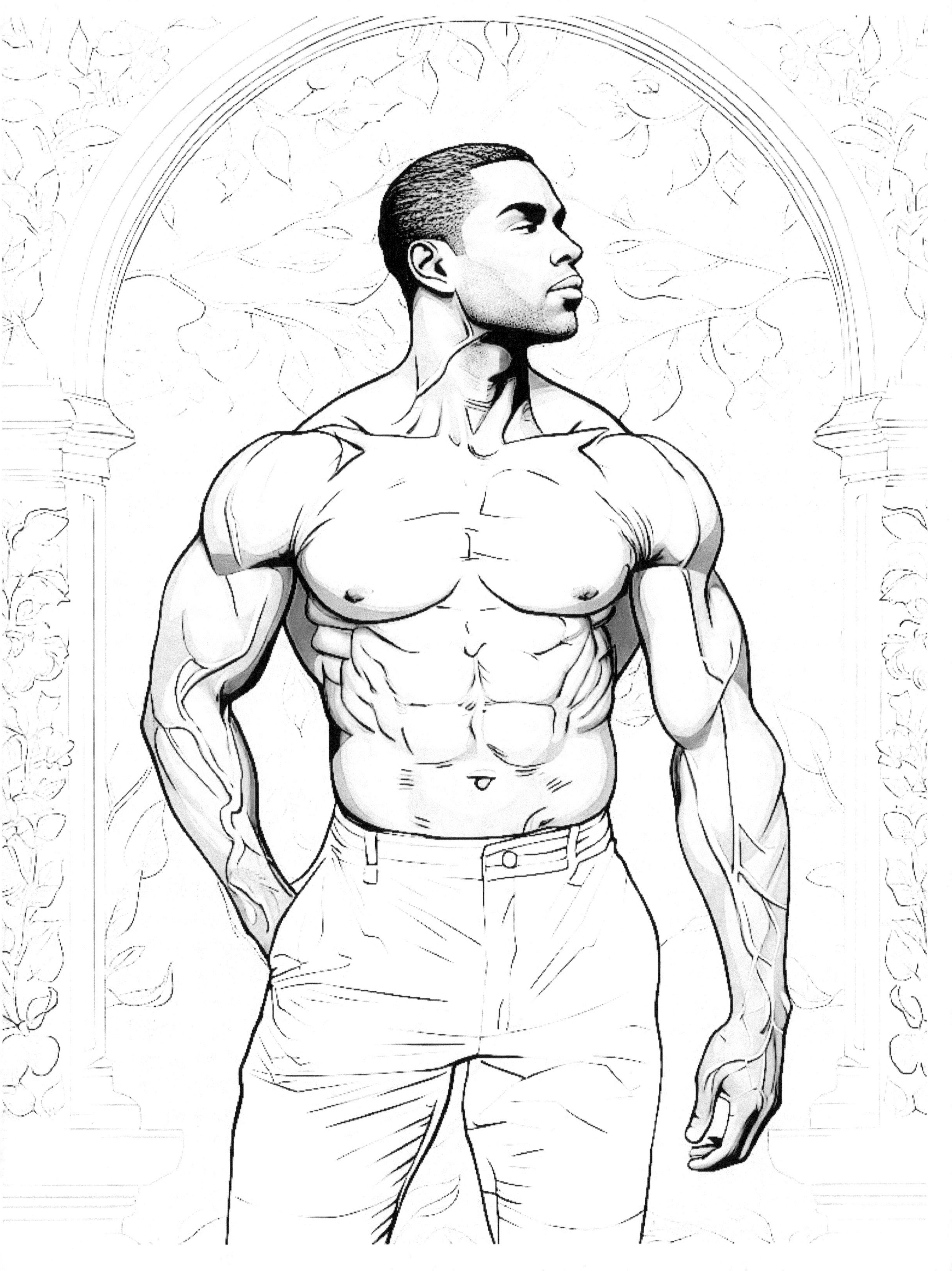

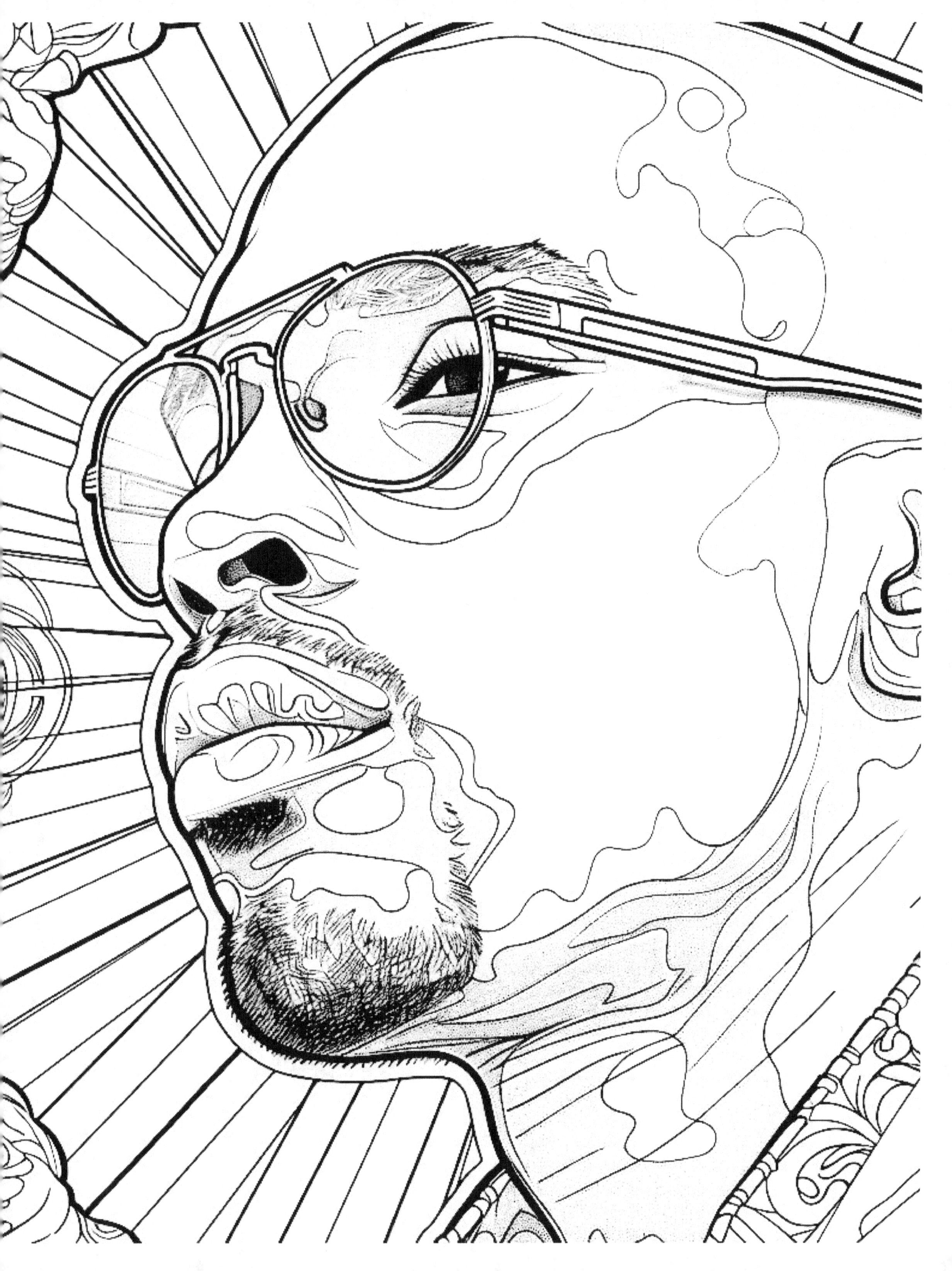

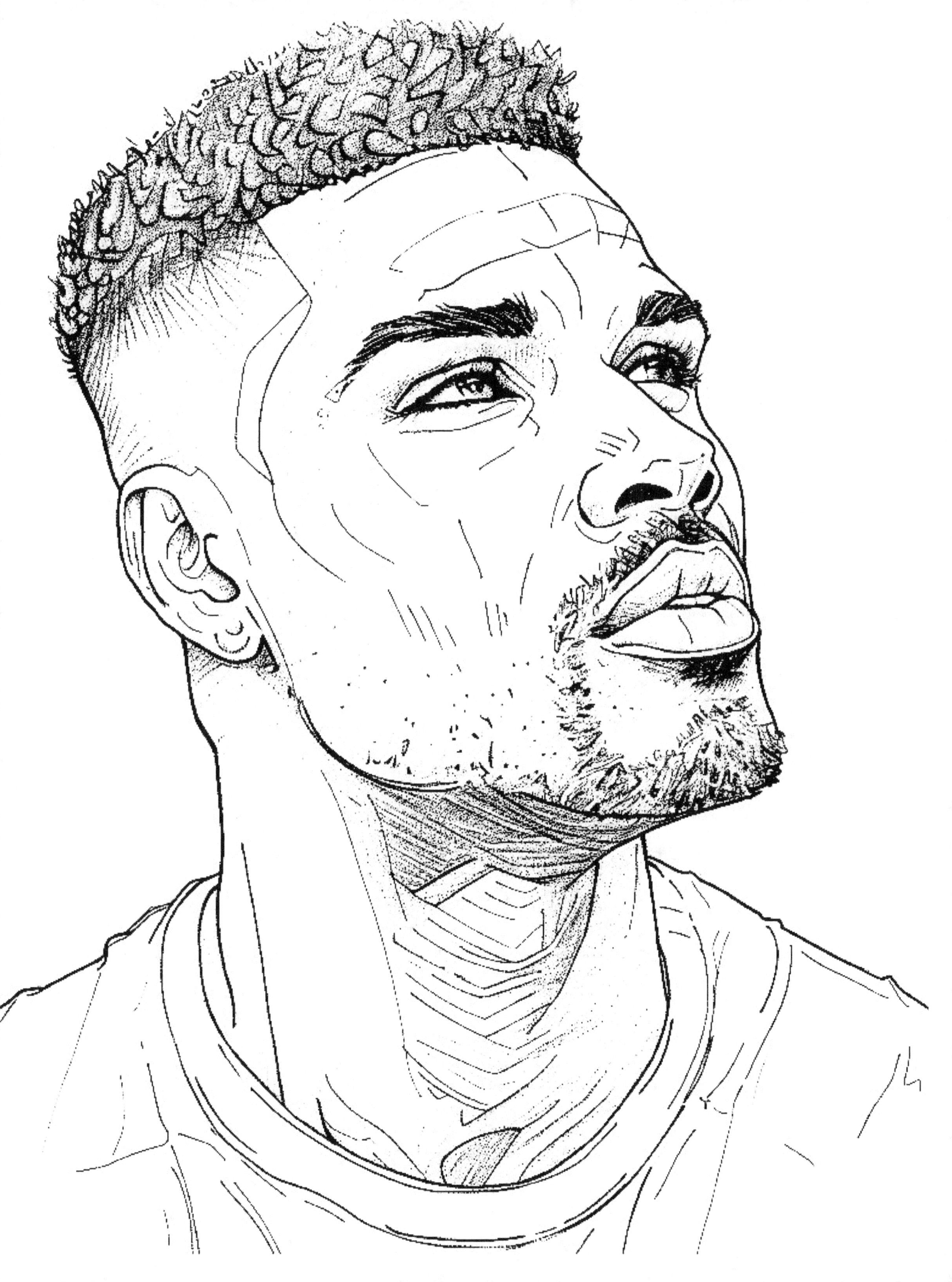

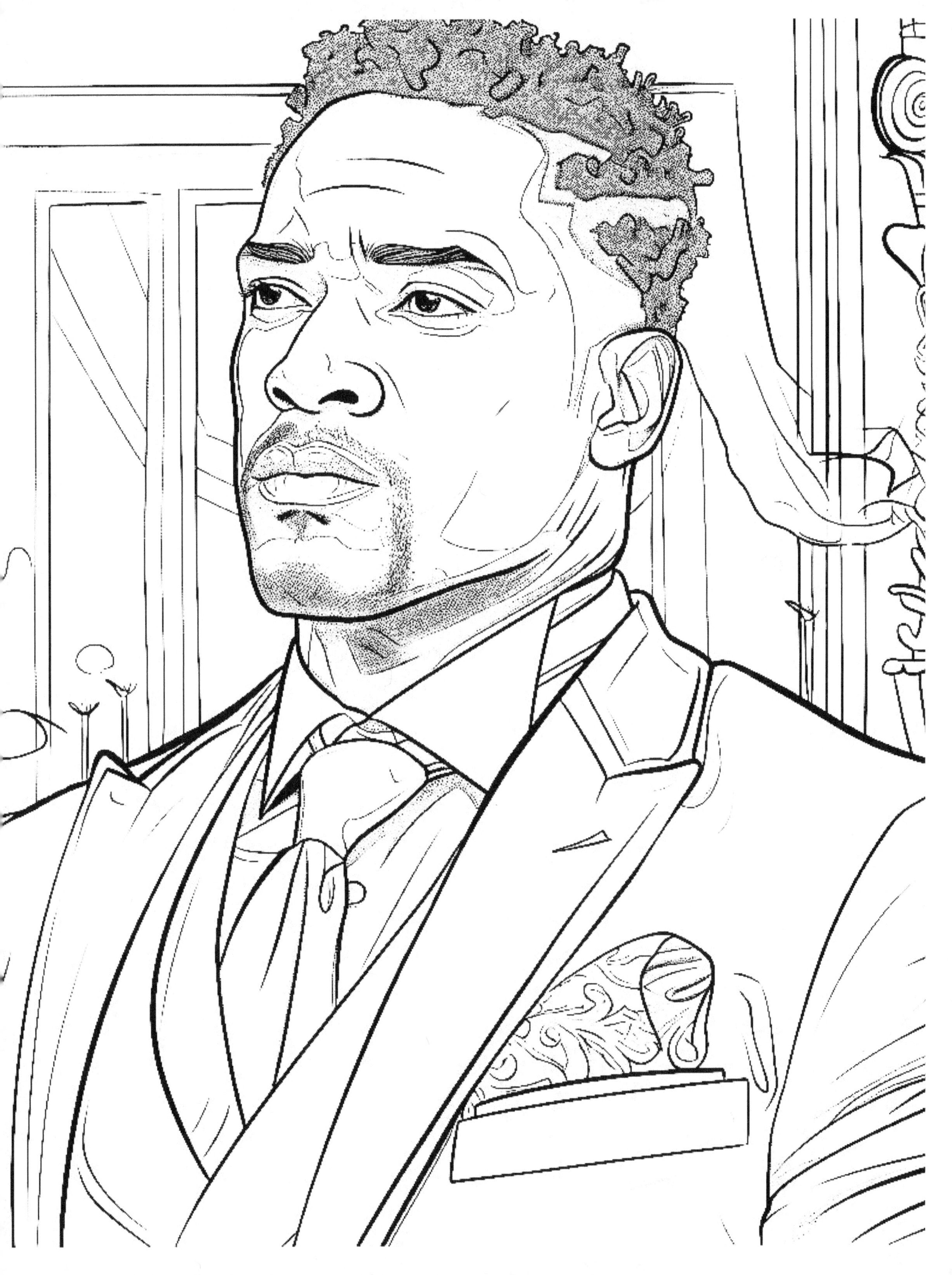

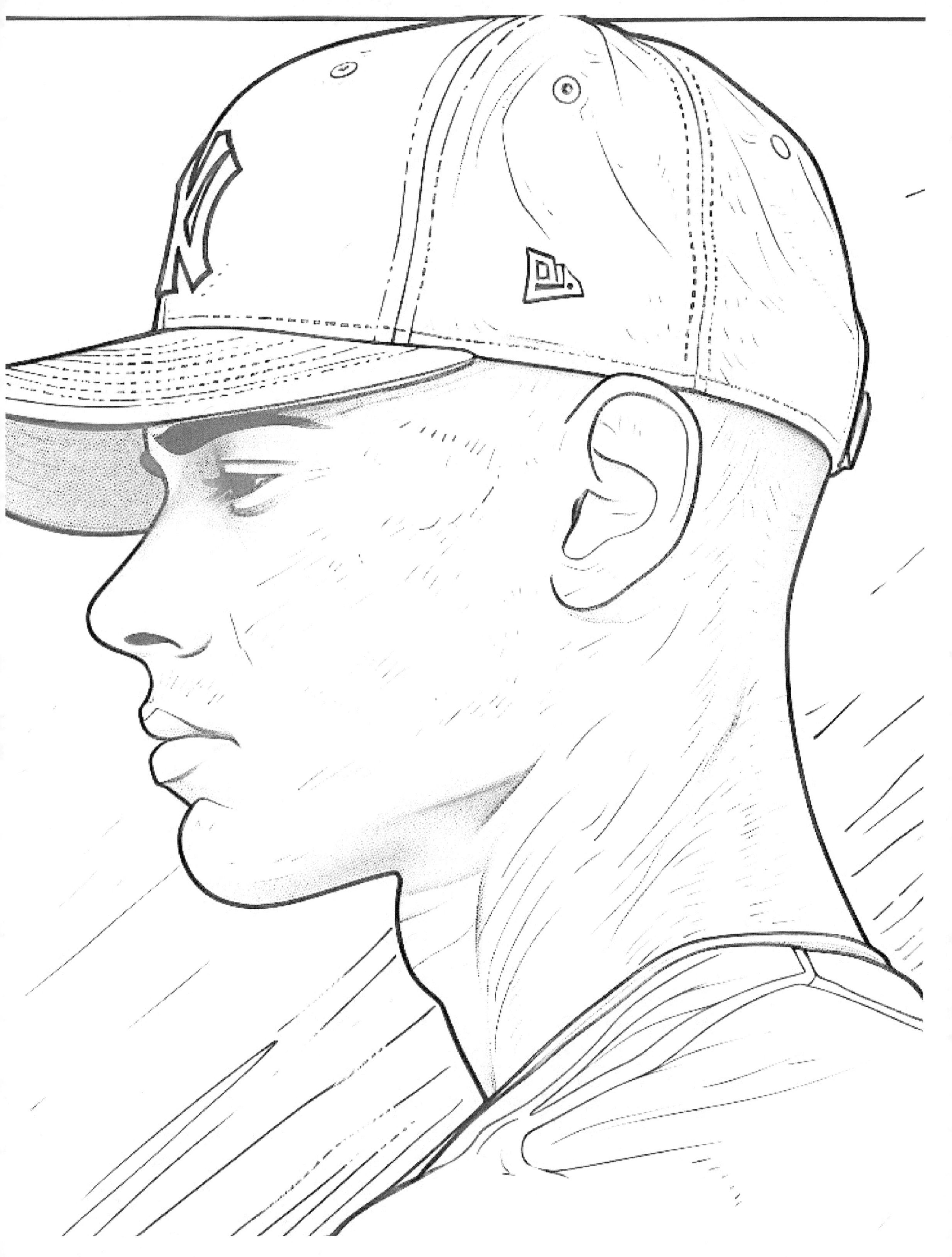

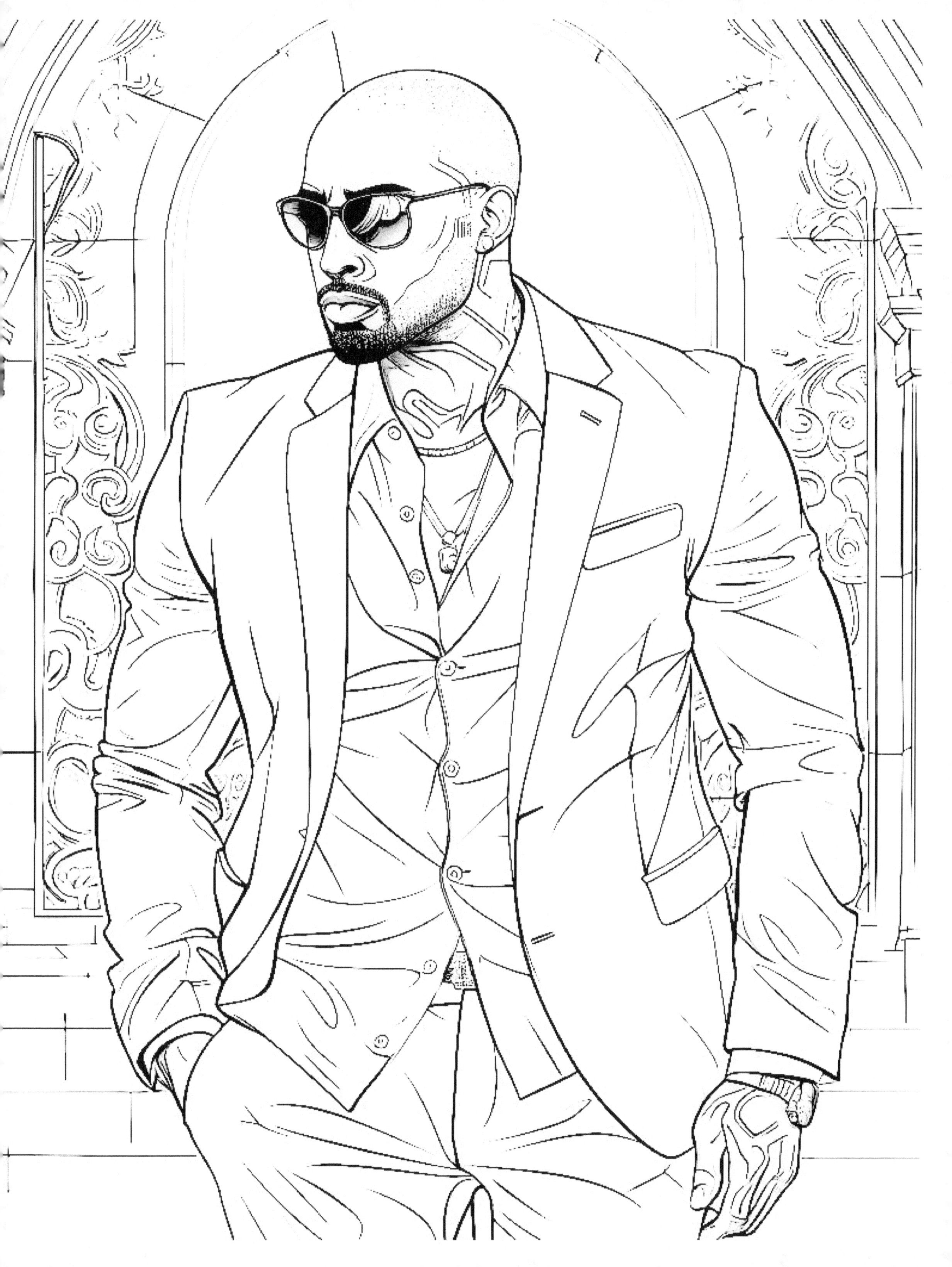

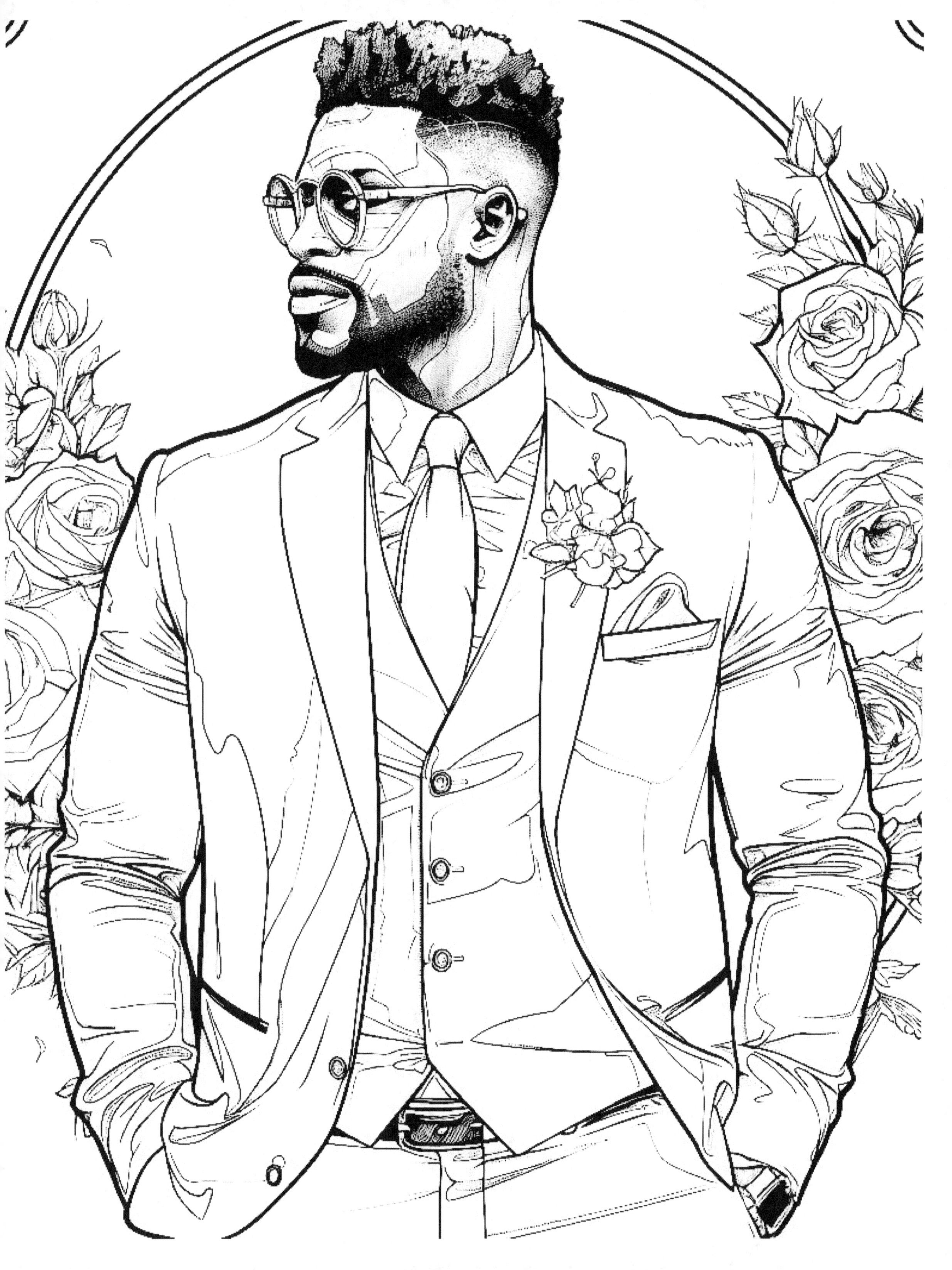

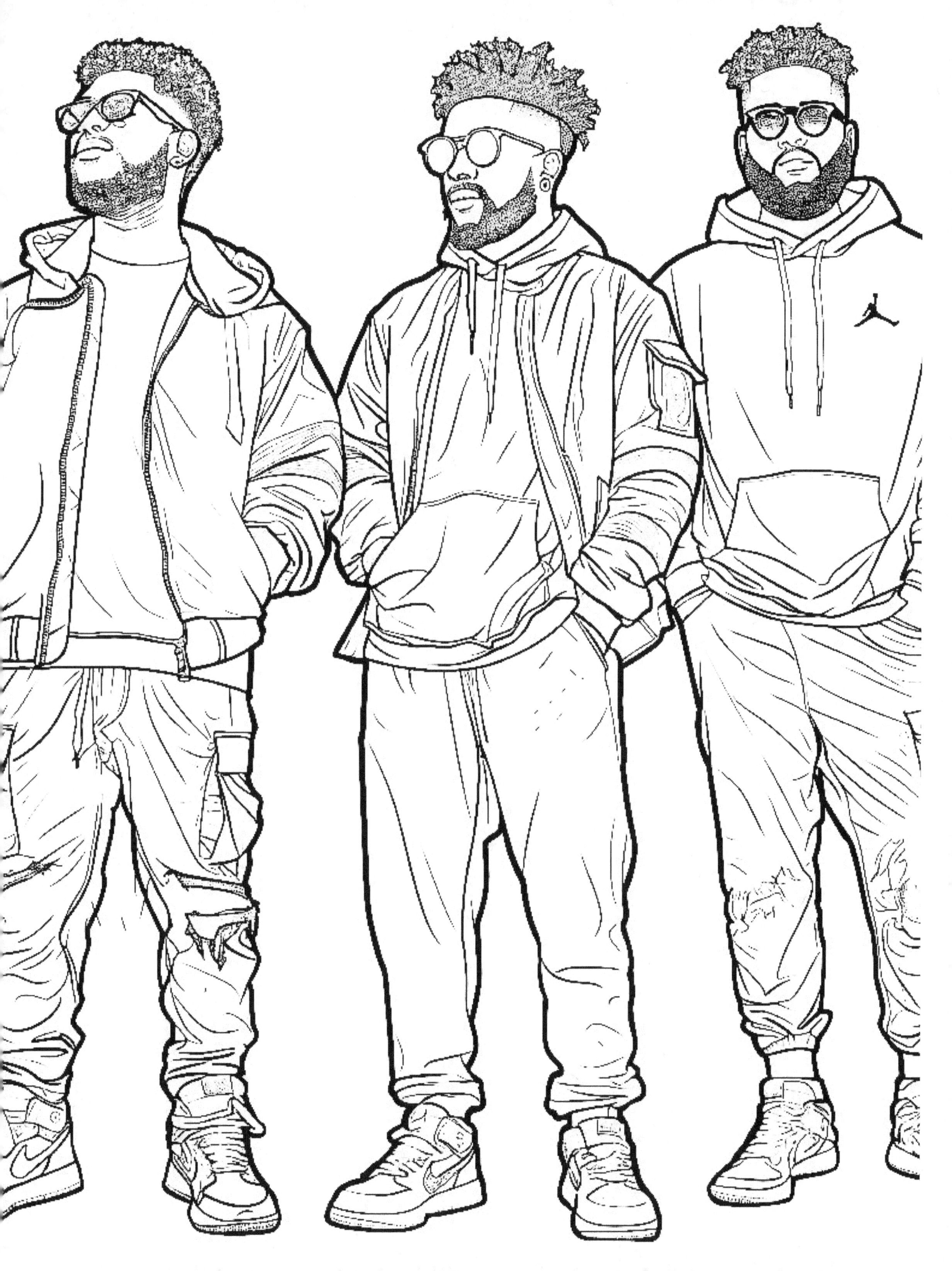

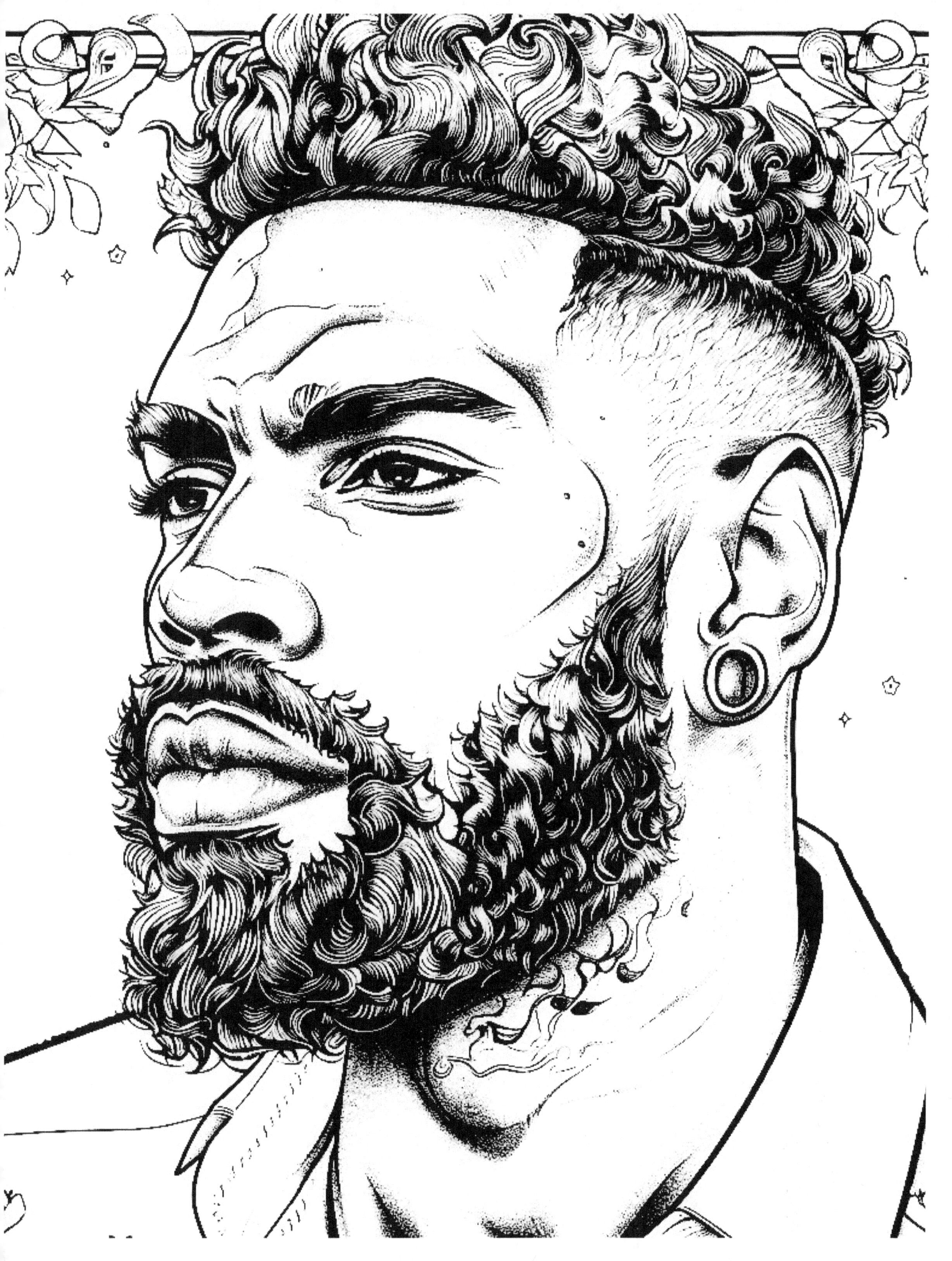

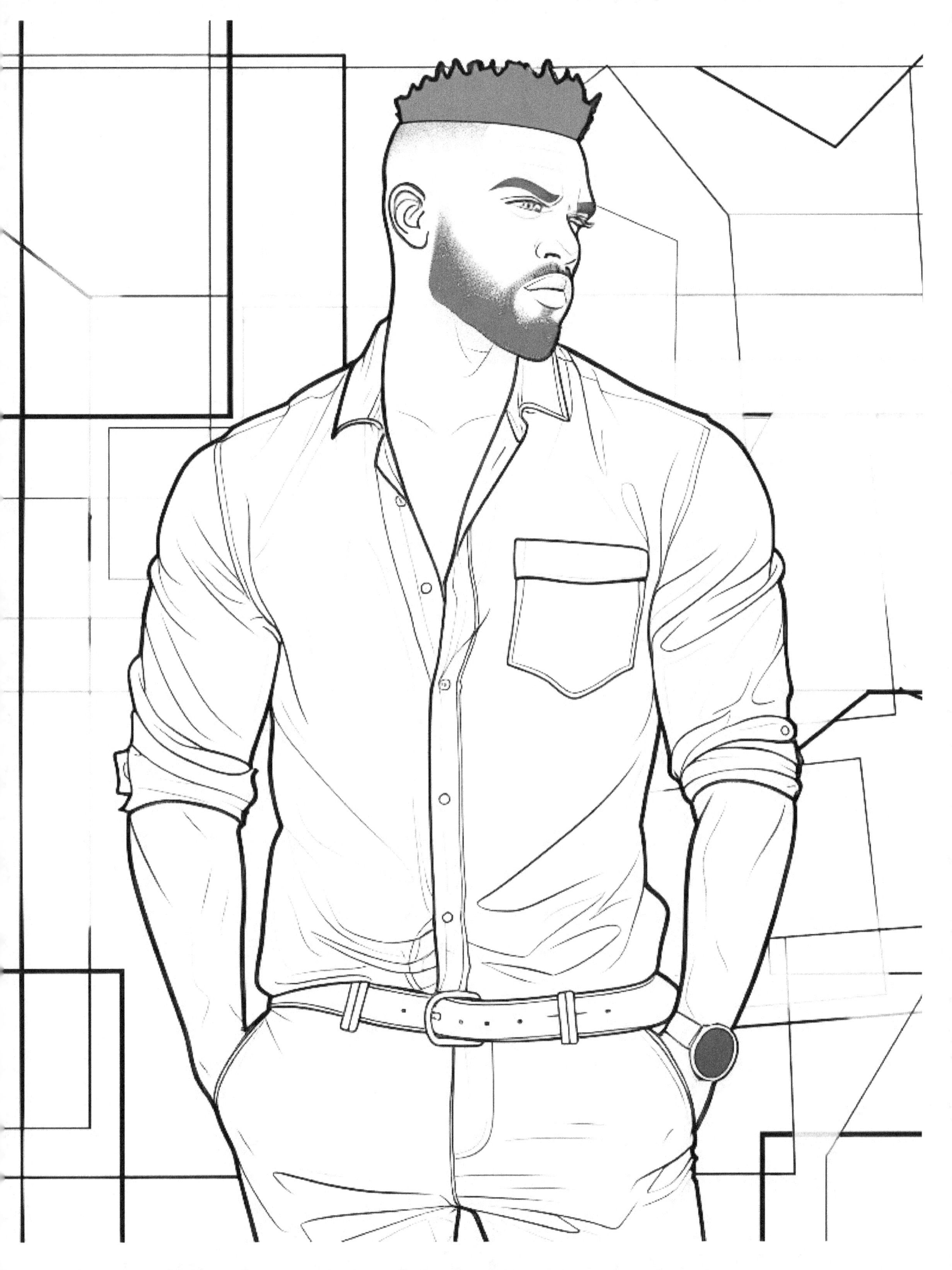

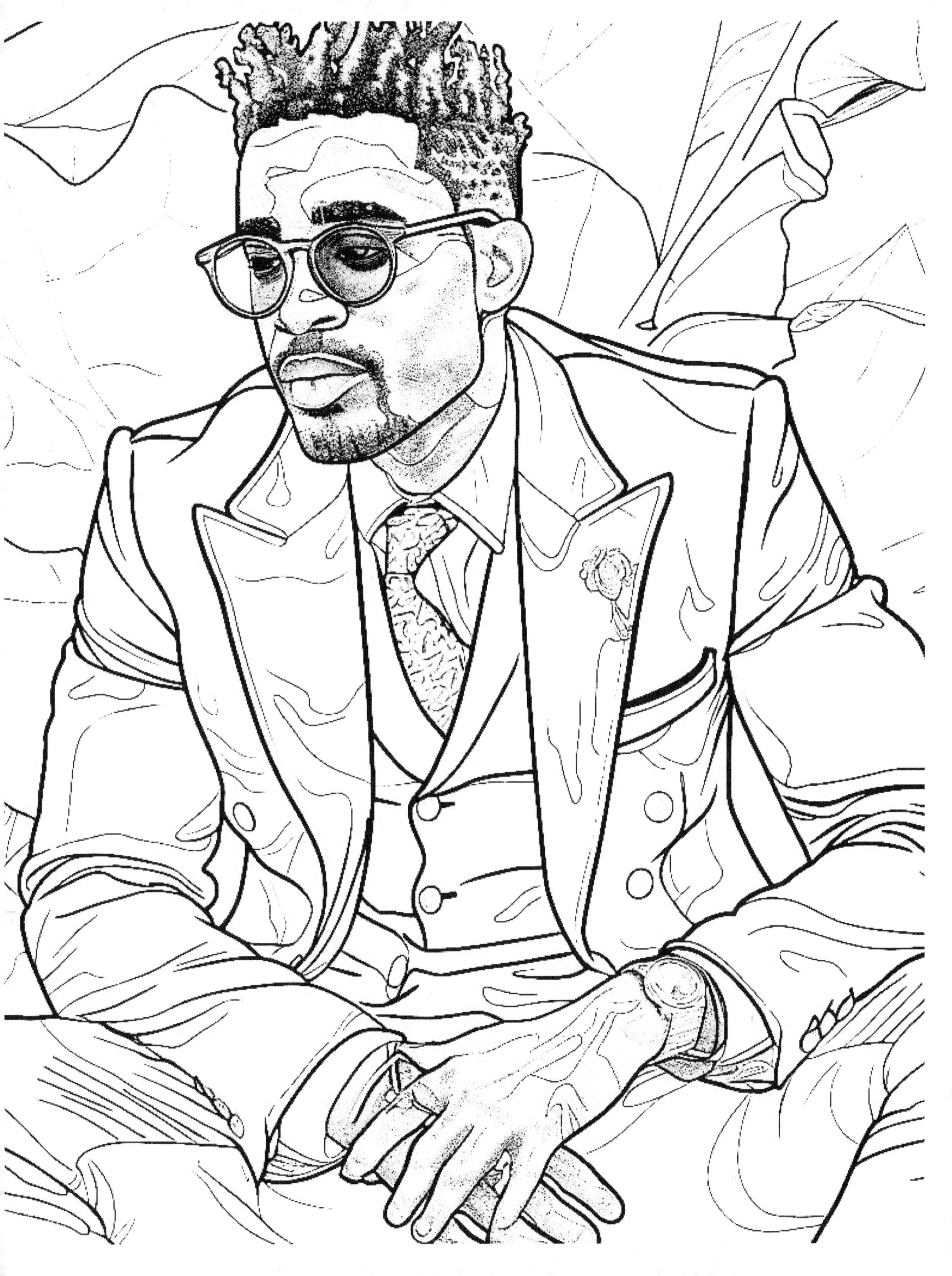

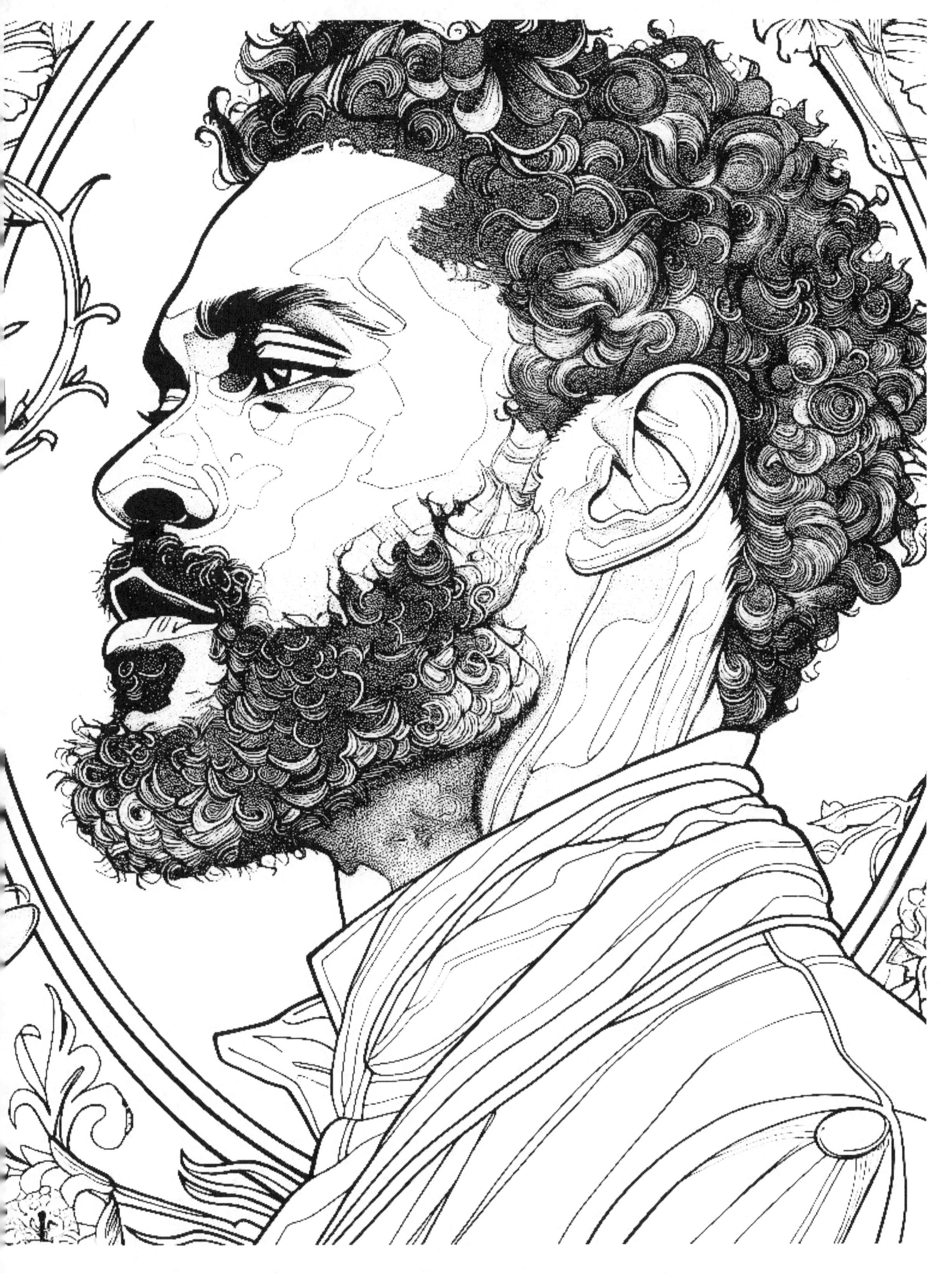

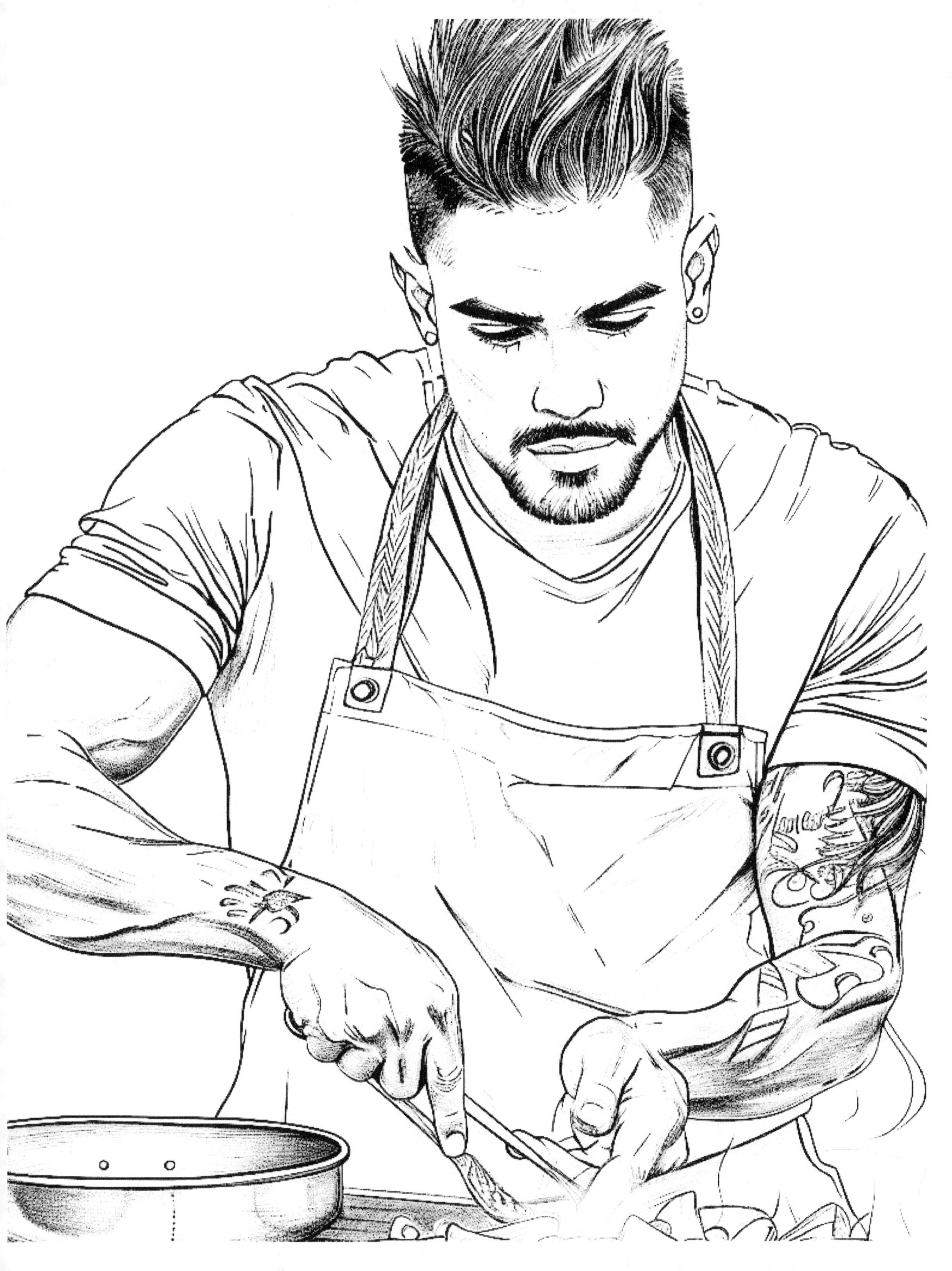

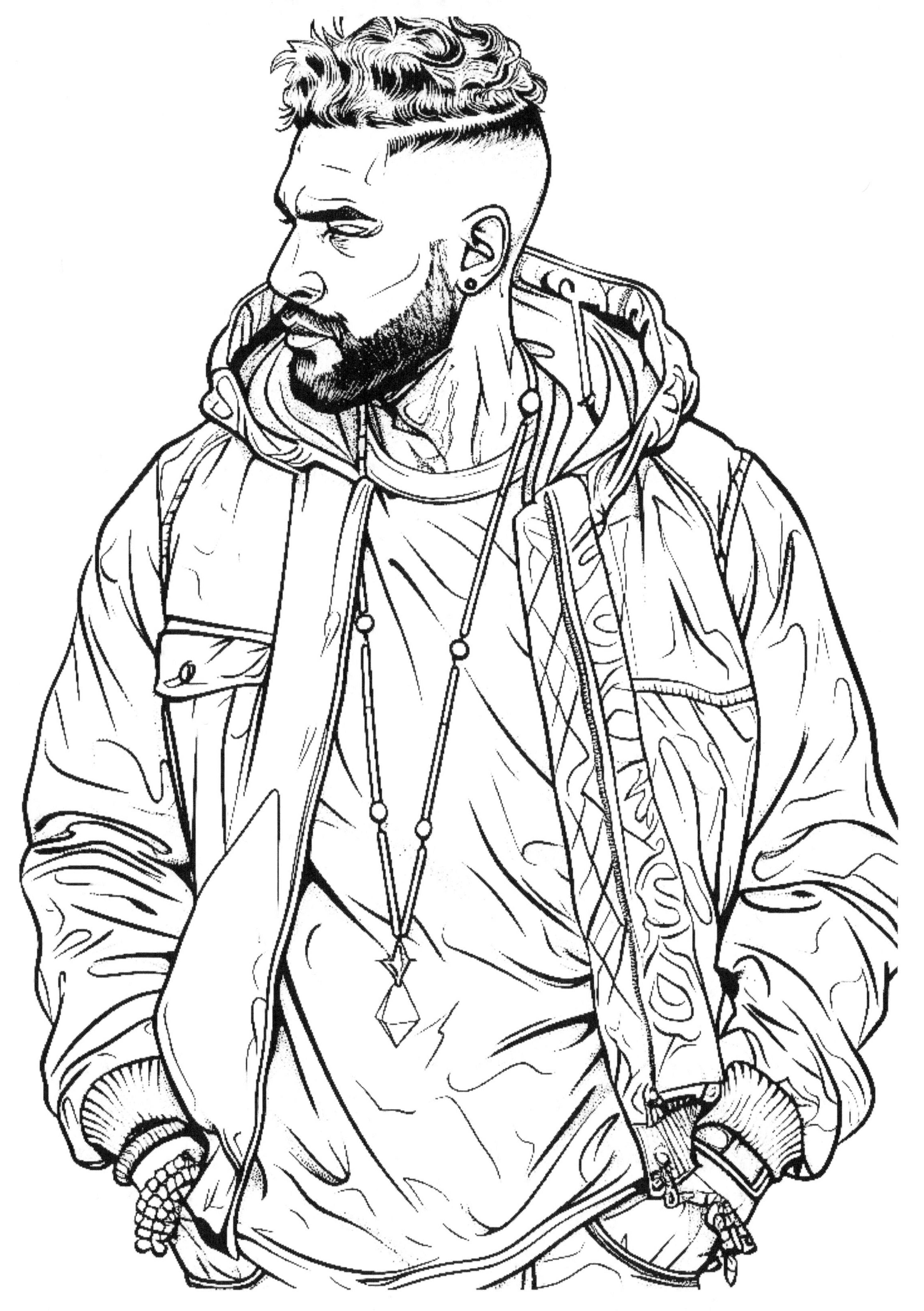

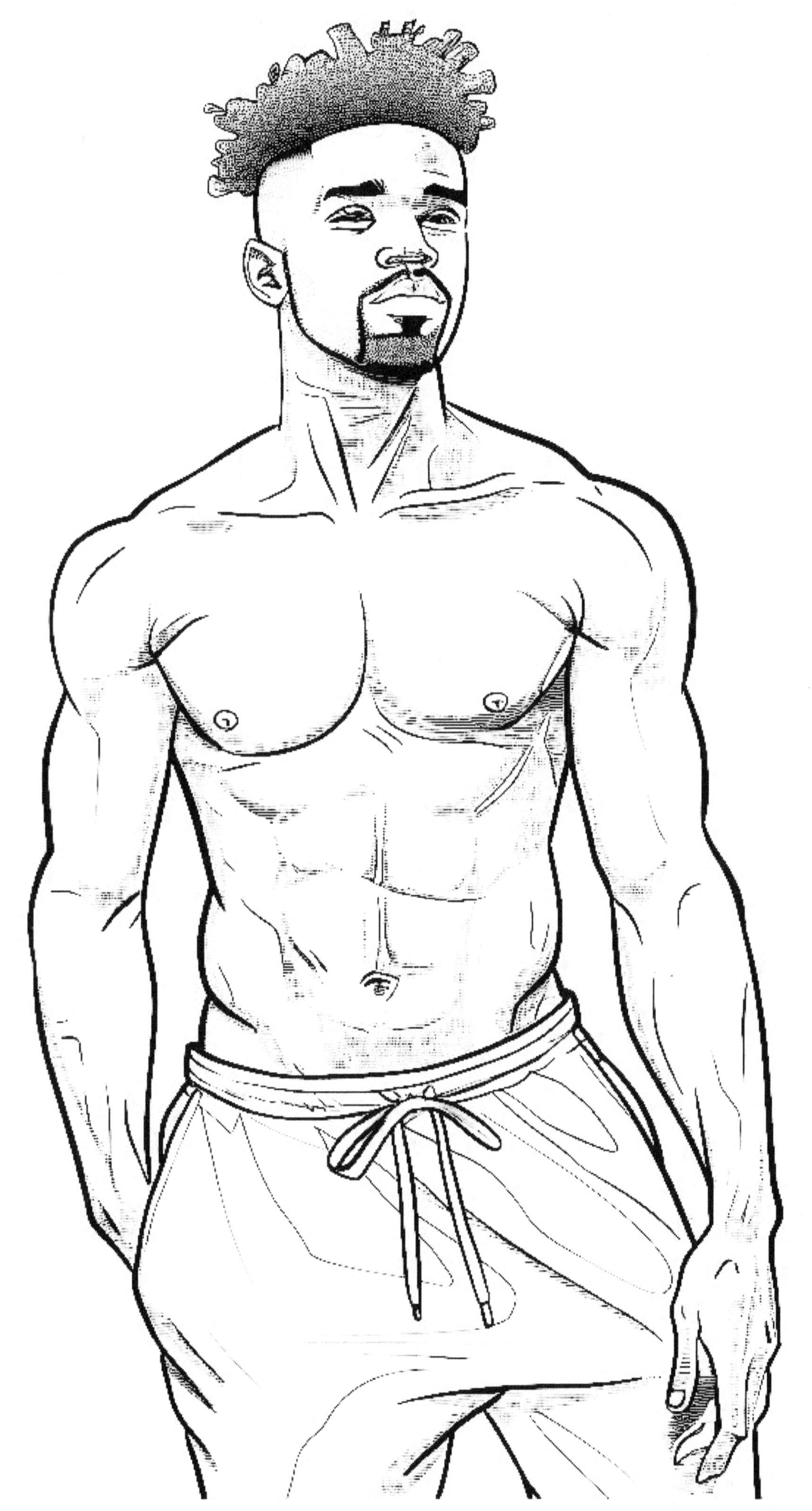

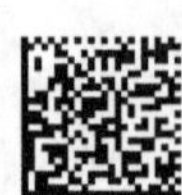